T0194881

LIFE-CHANGING
MOMENT

LAZARO S. GARCIA AKA SONNY

WESTBOW
PRESS®
A DIVISION OF THOMAS NELSON
& ZONDERVAN

WestBow Press books may be ordered through booksellers or by contacting:

WestBow Press
A Division of Thomas Nelson & Zondervan
1663 Liberty Drive
Bloomington, IN 47403
www.westbowpress.com
844-714-3454

ISBN: 978-1-6642-5381-0 (sc)
ISBN: 978-1-6642-5380-3 (e)

Library of Congress Control Number: 2021925666

Print information available on the last page.

WestBow Press rev. date: 2/25/2022

CONTENTS

1

PECUNIARY MATTER MINDSET

When 2018 was finally coming to an end, I was utterly determined to reestablish adequate, life-changing goals in my life. My only desire was to accomplish pivotal economic goals in 2019. I created an illusion in my mind that demonstrated my sincere desire to create a substantial and significant lifestyle. This imaginative lifestyle could only be achieved if I were able to demonstrate how successful I became in 2019. I wanted to show how I was able to become both rich and famous. I was certain that I was going to make 2019 significant and that it would be a substantial year that I would never forget, regardless of what would happen to me! Throughout everything that I had just gone through in 2018 which demonstrated how I had experienced significant financial struggles. All I ever wanted was to be able to achieve some financial success, which would not only reestablish my lifestyle but further ensure that I would never have to deal with any of the effects that come from a drastically low income.

I obtained a bachelor's degree in business administration with an emphasis in marketing in 2014. I was able to experience the lifestyle of having a significant amount of money. I even gained a full understanding of how money was made and lost. I would often feel arrogant, prideful, and full of self-exaltation knowing that I was the only person within my family ever to obtain such a substantial academic goal in that particular level of education.

My first job after achieving my bachelor's degree was at a car rental company, where I consistently reached the goal of making the most sales. I was even granted a three-day vacation in the city of Chicago, which was fully paid for by the car rental company.

Although I continuously achieved outstanding sales goals within that car rental company, I was frequently transferred to many locations within that city. And despite my achievements, they would not give me any monetary compensation or show appreciation for all the sales goals that I met and surpassed. It did not really matter where they placed me; sometimes they sent me to a private location within the city of El Paso or make me work at the airport location. No matter which location they sent me to, I surpassed all my fellow teammates when it pertained to the sales achievements.

I had been with that car rental company for over

three years and still not getting any type of advancement. Eventually I was offered an assistant manager position in a retail store that was located in a local mall in El Paso. I immediately accepted it. Not only did I accept the job offer at the retail store, I was able to persuade the human resources manager to give me a certain monetary compensation so I could leave the car rental company immediately. I was genuinely surprised that they accepted my terms.

I confess, however, that I did have some job management skills. But I still had many obstacles to overcome in order to be able to obtain and adapt to a new management position at a local retail store. In fewer than four months, they told me the retail store was going to close. Yet despite the fact that they had just given me horrific news, I was obligated to instruct and manage the employees within that retail store, at least until we sold all the items in stock. Every week they aspired to encourage shoppers and even tried to enact substantial marketing strategies that would make many local citizens want to buy more in the store. For example, they would reduce the price of the products by 10 percent. Each and every week they reduced the price another 10 percent until all the products in that store were sold out.

I was utterly unaware of any procedures or standards that I needed to follow, or at least participate in, to affect my life positively and ultimately release me from the difficult economic moment that I was experiencing. Despite my degree, it was still difficult to obtain a consistent job opportunity. So after much consideration and ceaseless effort, I decided to change my financial approach to one that would grant me the ability to retain monetary stability. After reading numerous books about financial success, I began to realize that they all repeated the same concepts again and again. They all stated that to retain any considerable monetary success, one should not spend his or her life just working effortlessly at any company for any type of monetary gain. Rather, everyone should insist on putting their monetary surplus into financial investments so that they can achieve financial stability solely through those investments.

Although I had extensive knowledge on how to manage people to achieve any particular goal, I was still uneducated about how and where I should invest my money. I began to notice that none of the books I read about finance was able to give me clear, proper instruction on how or where I should invest the little money I had left after the store had been fully shut down.

In that moment I purposefully decided it would be wise to meet with a financial adviser, who would be able to instruct me on where and how I should be investing my money. He would also instruct me on what I needed to do in order to perform. I also expected him to instruct me on what I should be doing with my money so that I would not have to work ever again and still be able to achieve financial success.

I spent countless hours trying to locate such a financial

adviser by using the internet and social media. But I still could not find any proper financial adviser. I then began to comb my memory to see if I remembered anyone with the proper education who had pursued a career in financial investments. Then I remembered that I had been going to a Christian church for many years, and there was a member who had earned a degree in finance and then created his own business in financial advising.

Once I was able to recollect all the particular thoughts I had of him, I looked him up on the internet. I just wanted to see if there was any information pertaining to him. Once I was able to locate the information about his business and its location, I called him and arranged a meeting so he could educate me in financial investments.

2

CASO PERDIDO

(Lost Cause)

There had been minimum communication between Mr. Andrew and I at our local church. I'd faithfully attended a local Christian church and met him when he was attending a high school academy while I was still in fifth grade. There was an immense age difference between us. Nevertheless, I was excited to start my investment journey.

I decided that it would be best to retrieve any information I previously had about Mr. Andrew so there would be better communication between us. Although I had once been a local church member, in that moment I had begun to analyze my personal life and realized how I had begun slowly and one step at a time to leave out the importance of who God was in my life. I'd gradually begun to stray from God and His divine commandments that are stated throughout the Bible. I slowly, yet some will say miraculously, stepped away from the Almighty God, so slightly that no one would ever notice. I further became more enthralled with certain lifestyle pleasures and satisfactions that eventually, all the decisions I made led me step away from God completely.

I was able to see Mr. Andrew on several occasions. He kept politely insisting on informing me that the primary function of the business he created was to help people release themselves from massive debt situations and further, to help them to initialize a budget. Once he was able to get the individual to that financial goal, he would coach them on how they should be spending their money. He asked me to describe my current financial situation. After, due to the fact that I still had not gone too deeply into debt, he informed me it would be best to start investing.

After having several meetings with him, I arranged to see him one more time, at 4:00 p.m. on February 15, 2019, at his business location. I remember waking up that day and thinking that it was a beautiful, lovely day.

Because I had lost my job at the retail store, I began to live at my grandmother's old mobile home, located in the city of Las Cruces. I quickly figured out how much time it would take for me to get to Mr. Andrew's office in time for our appointment. I decided to leave the mobile home approximately ninety minutes before the arranged time frame so I would arrive on time.

It was approximately 3:30 p.m., and I was driving east on the freeway and was near an exit. Then suddenly I noticed this large black truck was driving westbound in such a crazy, maniacal fashion. As I kept driving on freeway heading east bound, I kept noticing how he continued to drive in such a strange fashion. I believed he would eventually regain his mentality and consciousness and drive in a normal fashion. As both time and miles passed, his driving became increasingly erratic. Then without any warning, he began driving straight toward me.

I quickly reacted. I thought it would be a good idea if I accelerated in the hope of avoiding the truck by speeding out of his way. But in that specific moment, I was blocked by a vehicle in front of me and unable to speed away. The truck driver broke through the metal barrier that separated the westbound and eastbound traffic, went through the ditch, hit a white truck, and then completely landed atop my vehicle.

And in that particular moment, after being involved in a severe car accident, my brain and my memory surely began to fade. Even though I wanted to recall what had just happened to me, I was unable to remember anything completely because I had been injured so severely. Yet, despite these severe circumstances, I can slightly remember that within minutes after the accident, I could hear a strong, powerful female voice coming from outside my vehicle telling me repeatedly, "Stay with me now," "Don't leave."

With everything I experienced that day, I can slightly remember hearing how people tried to pull me out of my vehicle. But despite their continued efforts, they could not fully open the car door because the car door had been severely damaged. I can also remember that within minutes, the fire department showed up. They were the only ones able to break the car door open, so they could pull me out of the vehicle. I slightly remember how they put me on a stretcher, placed an oxygen mask over my mouth and nose, and I lost consciousness.

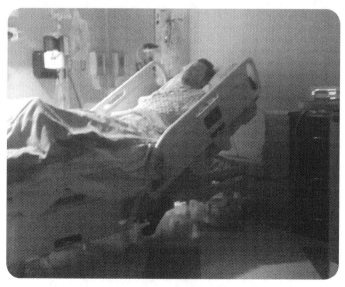

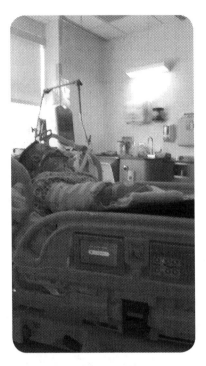

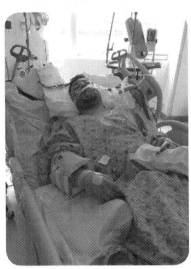

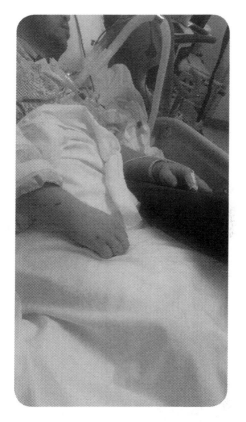

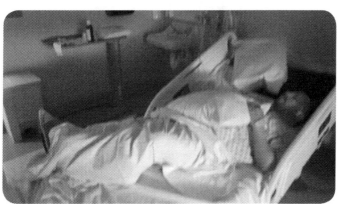

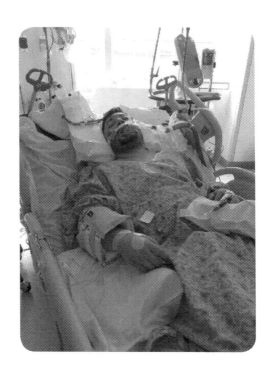

Field Diagram - Not to Scale

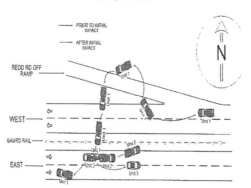

INTERSTATE 10 MILE MARKER 10

Not To Scale

3

ICU, El Paso, TX

As I had been involved in a serious car accident, the information in this chapter was provided to me by my parents. My mother provided me with most of its contents, so it will be much easier to read. This chapter is told from her perspective, as if she were the one speaking.

I decided to schedule an appointment with a nail technician late in the afternoon on that Friday. This was something that I was not accustomed to doing; I always scheduled my nail appointments early in the morning or early in the afternoon. Yet for some reason, on February 15, 2019, my nail appointment was scheduled for 5:30 p.m.

On that particular day I actually left the nail salon late because I stayed several minutes in order to help my technician clean up. I quickly called my husband to inform him that I was heading home. Prior to arriving home, I decided to stop at a grocery store to pick up several items. I called my husband again to tell him I was heading home at that particular moment.

Once I had arrived home, I headed towards my bedroom. Then I heard a knock on my door. At first I hesitated, but then I heard it again. In that moment, I quickly decided that I was not going to answer the door as I did not expect anyone. But for some strange reason, I changed my mind and decided to open the door. A sheriff's vehicle was in the process of leaving my home. A female officer heard me open the front door and headed straight toward me. I thought, *I do not remember Sonny ever applying for the sheriff's department.*

While I was still considering that option, she interrupted my train of thought. "I am looking for the next of kin for a man by the name of Lazaro S. Garcia."

I was immediately filled with total shock. I quickly responded, "I am his mother." I was so shocked. I could not even move in order to contact my husband! I finally gained enough strength to call him, yet he would not answer; it seemed to be as if he were on the other line. Although it was only minutes, it seemed to me like forever. I was still unable to move.

The officer quickly said, "Ma'am, I need to see your identification."

I stated, "My purse is right there." With all that was occurring to me in that particular moment, I still was not able to get in communication with my husband. Then I remembered that he was at my mother-in-law's house with my brother-in-law. In that perplexing moment, I decided to leave him a message. After waiting several minutes, he returned my call. I quickly told him, "Sonny is in the ICU, and you need to come home now!"

I asked the female officer, "Would you please stay inside the home and wait until my husband arrives so I can get to the ICU?"

She kindly yet sternly replied, "No! We do not need another accident at this moment." Considering the situation, I finally sat down. The female officer gave me the phone number of a social worker at the hospital. The social worker quickly notified me that I needed to get to the hospital as quickly as possible. I told her we lived approximately forty-five minutes away! My husband still had not arrived. The social worker told me I should come quickly.

Although maybe only a couple of minutes had passed, it seemed like forever. My husband finally arrived. He quickly changed shoes, and we headed to the hospital. It seemed to me as if we were only driving approximately fifteen miles per hour. Along the way to the hospital I was continually crying and praying. I thought that it would be a great idea to text my current prayer group so that they can begin to pray for my son. Yet I was so stunned by the entire situation that I could not even text.

My husband told me to investigate and see if there was anything on the news. So I looked on Google to see if there was any information about the accident. Suddenly I saw my son's severely damaged car on the front page of the news. I was so devastated by the notification that was being displayed on the news that I began to yell uncontrollably. I even began to hit the passenger window, but I didn't break anything.

I immediately began to call out to the Lord. A startling peace immediately came over me, and I was then able to maintain stillness. I prayed, "Lord, if Sonny has accepted you as his Lord and Savior, please give us strength because for any parent, it is hard to lose a child. If Sonny still has not committed his life to You and accepted You as his Lord and Savior, please grant him one more opportunity."

When we finally arrived at the hospital, we quickly found the ICU section. During this whole time, I felt like I was floating. A nurse at the front desk of the ICU was waiting for us and opened the door. While my husband and I headed toward our son, a nurse stopped us. She told us we would not be able to proceed any further because they had not been able to identify him. I told her, "I can immediately identify him. I fully recognize that those are my son's feet and hands."

As I began to walk around the nurse, I saw how his eyes were halfway opened and glazed over. I reached out and touched his left arm. It felt like it was colder than ice. My husband came closer, I told him, "That's it. We've lost him!"

As soon as my son heard the sound of my voice, he

miraculously started to raise his right arm. I genuinely believe he was giving us a sign telling us, "Do not give up." I strongly believe that the sign also was coming from the Lord. I concluded that my son was not yet saved, and God was giving him yet another opportunity.

Many nurses started to ask my husband a lot of questions. To be honest, I cannot recall what they were for because I was still in complete shock. While my husband was taking care of many things, such as the insurance and answering questions, I stayed next to my son, just letting him know that we were there for him.

After constantly pleading for information I began searching for the social worker that I had spoken with previously over the phone. To this day, I have not been able to meet her or even know what she looks like. Yet I will confidently say that this social worker never gave up on searching for our child's family members. She kept insisting to the police officers to search over and over again. They first sent a unit to our son's address located in Las Cruces, and no one was there. The officers were finally able to find another address, which was our home, and they sent a sheriff's deputy to our home.

My husband was still trying to get any information to better understand what occurred. Our church family began to arrive at the hospital. Besides all the calling and texting that was going on, I had to leave our son's bedside to meet with family members. Surprisingly, all our family began to show up! We still had to decide how we should call our other son and daughter, who were living in a different part of the state. It was getting late, so I went back to the ICU to be with my son and husband. I pulled two chairs together because I was not leaving our son's room.

It was shift change at the hospital when I overheard the nurse updating a nurse coming on duty. "The patient does not remember. We are still considering him an unidentified being who was involved in severe car accident and suffering with blood pressure … He may be paralyzed on the left side, but he reacted when he was getting stitched up." After that I was unable to hear anything else for I was solely focused on praising the Lord for healing our son.

Hours later, a neurologist called my husband and I, so we could go over a CT scan performed on our son. I could easily see a lot of white spots. The neurologist explained to us that those white spots were blood spots. The neurologist stated that our son was bleeding in the brain, and there were also blood spots within the brain stem. Another person explained to us that no one was willing to do surgery when it comes to the brain stem. I smiled and quickly said, "His Creator can and will!" She continued to explain our child's condition, and I just kept smiling.

She then recommended a procedure that would give them the opportunity to better understand our son's brain movement. They wanted to drill a hole in his skull so they would be able to get more information. In my heart and mind, I was yelling, *Yeah right. No way.* My husband asked them if our son had any liquid in his brain. They quickly answered no. My husband gracefully told her that we needed to pray about it.

As we headed back to our son's room, we were greeted by a group of distinguished doctors intently looking at his right foot. They scheduled an X-ray right away. When the results came in, it showed that his right foot was shattered yet amazingly still intact. They told us that they needed to perform surgery on his foot right away. I did not want that to happen because I was fully aware that the anesthesia they would have to give him could affect our son's brain. The anesthesia would begin to slow brain activity, and I did not want that. My husband told them we needed to talk about it as a family as our other children had just already arrived.

I was being so negative and told my husband no. Yet a sister in Christ told him it was particularly important for our son to have the surgery. So the next morning my husband told me to look for the doctor and inform him to go ahead with our son's surgery. He solely meant the foot surgery. I spoke to the neurologist and told her to go ahead and move forward with the procedure she wanted to do. She looked at me and politely said, "We did another CT scan on him, and the swelling that was in his brain has gone down. We actually no longer have to do the procedure."

I immediately began to state, "Praise the Lord," and called my husband, who had gone home to get some rest, and told him. He stopped me and said, "You needed to look for the doctor and let her know about the surgery on his foot!"

I began to question myself: *Was all of this a mix-up?* I genuinely did not think so. I honestly believed—and continue to believe—that God was in totally control! I kept thinking, *Oh, man, I messed up!* But God knew exactly what He was doing. So I immediately went to go look for the podiatrist to see what was going to be done regarding our son's surgery on his foot. I could not find the doctor. When I got back to our son's room, the podiatrist was waiting there in his room. She quickly told me that my son's bones were miraculously healing from the inside-out, which meant he would not need any surgery. "Praise the Lord," I kept claiming.

As I continually thanking the Lord, my tears would simply just come out. I was so amazed at how He was consistently answering my prayers. I particularly remember calling out to the Lord, thanking Him for the fact that we still had our son on this earth. I remember telling Him, "Lord, thank You because my son is still alive. Even though he might not be able to see through his left eye, I am OK with that. But I do not know how our son will react to that! Lord, let Your will be done."

It was my turn to go home and rest, and I was ready to take a nap. My cell phone suddenly began to ring; it was my husband. I got so scared! He informed me that the eye specialist had come in, and our son would still be able to see with his left eye. Our son was suffering with a lot of dry blood behind his eye. I was so amazed that I began to weep in joy for I knew that our son would be able to see with both eyes once again. Praise You, Lord!

Through all the ups and downs and the decisions that we needed to make, I kept reminding myself that no one, absolutely no one, would be able to take my faith from Jesus Christ. No one! Not even me. I thank the Lord for what He did and what He continues to do in my son's life and in ours.

4

MISS JENNIFER

After my accident on February 15, 2019, a woman by the name of Miss Jennifer contacted my parents. She told them she was a registered nurse who had been involved and witnessed the accident. My parents and I thought it be prudent to meet with her. So December 27, 2019, we met with her at a local pizza restaurant. Push comes to shove, we at least had the opportunity to thank her for the services she provided that day.

At first, I will fully admit I was extremely shy about what happened to me. I was also shy because I was still undergoing rehabilitation as I was unable to perform as before my accident. I was still walking in an awkward, weird fashion. There were so many things I still did not know how to ask her about what she experienced and saw on February 15, 2019.

When our pizza order was ready, my parents went to the counter to pick it up. In that moment I was left alone with Miss Jennifer, something happened within me that helped me to gain enough confidence to ask her, "So what happened? What did you see?"

She politely responded, "Every single day I am always exceeding the speed limit so that I get to at the location I need to be. Every single time I drive my vehicle, I tend to speed. It allows me to get rid of the unnecessary stress and tension that I usually experience because of all the traffic. On that particular day, however, I was driving slowly for some reason. I noticed that I had so much time before I had to be at work, so I suddenly decided to buy everyone at my job different coffees from a local coffee shop. I had so much free time that I could stop at my job, ask everyone their preferred coffee flavors, go to the coffee shop, buy the coffee, head back to work, and still get back to work just on time.

"While I was driving toward my work, I noticed this black truck driving in a strange manner near an exit off the freeway. I thought that maybe he had missed his exit and was going to drive to the next one. Then I saw him change his direction that would inevitably head straight toward you. All this happened in a matter of seconds. I saw him break through the metal barrier, go through the ditch, hit a truck, and land on top of your vehicle.

"I immediately stopped, got out of my vehicle, and headed straight toward the truck to make sure he was all right. Just as I began to ask him if he was all right, the driver began cussing. I didn't have any time to think, so I told him,

'You know what? Forget you. I have to go to the other small vehicle and see how they are doing.' I quickly ran toward your vehicle. As I arrived, you were gasping for air, like as if you couldn't breathe. I quickly began telling you 'Stay with me now!' Don't leave me!' 'Just stay with me now!' 'Do not leave me now!'

"I was seriously frightened about everything that had happened. I even started to get nervous about the fact that you could actually die at any given moment. I was so traumatized by the accident that I refused to drive my car anywhere for a whole week. I even begged my mother to take me to and from work. I refused to drive on that same road altogether for another month. It has and will continue to be a pivotal moment that I will never forget."

I was genuinely so amazed at all the information that she had just given me about what she witnessed that specific day. I did not have the words to describe how I felt at that moment. When my parents got back with the pizzas, I took a bite, but I was so affected by Miss Jennifer's story that I did not want to eat more of the pizza.

I was genuinely amazed by all the information that I had received. My brain did not have the ability to contemplate it all. After receiving all this information, I still had to go to a rehabilitation hospital and through many procedures and activities in order to try to regain my abilities so I could get back to my former self.

5

MRS. SHERI OT AND MRS. TATIANA SLP

I was not sure what to do with all the information I learned from Miss Jennifer. I had an enlightening meeting with a lawyer by the name of Mr. Nevarez. He was going to represent me in my case and do it totally pro bono. I admit, I was extremely grateful to have a lawyer represent me in the court of law free of charge. For the first time in my life, I was genuinely speechless. I seriously did not have any words to say. I still could not fully comprehend how I was in an accident or how severe the consequences were. I could not even remember how or where it had happened to me. I was sincerely confused because of the traumatic brain injury (TBI) I received in the accident.

I was still fortunate enough to be going to the rehabilitation hospital in Las Cruces. I still had to go through continuous progression exercises. But I was blessed to be transferred from inpatient status to outpatient.

As a result of the accident, I was severely damaged on the left side of my body. I was barely able to walk, having a very bad limp in my left leg. My left hand would not work properly either. After considering all the traumatic injuries I endured, the most difficult was fully recovering the use of my left eye. It was nearly impossible to even open my left eye.

I was fortunately assigned to an occupational therapist at the rehabilitation hospital by the name of Mrs. Sheri. During one of my first assignments with her, I asked her if she could please help me to recover my memory. I told her, "I know I am traveling from El Paso to Las Cruces because I am staying at my parents' house due to the accident. They were taking me to the rehabilitation hospital every Tuesday and Thursday because those were the only days they were able to get off work. But every time we headed toward Las Cruces, it seemed like I was going to a completely different country. Everywhere I go seems to be entirely brand new to me, like someone is entirely taking me to a whole different location in the world where I have never been before. Everything seems completely new to me because my brain cannot remember anything."

My brain had been so severely damaged that I could not even recall what happened to my vehicle. Then one day when I was with my mother at a gas station, I saw someone driving a vehicle that looked exactly like mine—the same make, color, and rims. It was in that moment my memory slowly started to come back to me.

Mrs. Sheri looked at me politely and yet firmly stated, "Get up, and take a look at your entire body. Start with your feet, and go all the way up to your head. You see, when the body decides to begin repairing itself, that is the order its reconstruction will begin. So, your body will first start on your feet; your body is recovering from a fractured foot. Then it will begin to reconstruct your legs. Your body will then begin transitioning to start repairing another part of your body. This process will continue until your whole body being fully reconstructed.

"Once your body has taken any necessary measures to be able to reconstruct your middle body, it will begin to reconstruct your arms. Once all those body parts have been reconstructed, your body will finally begin to reconstruct your head."

Then she asked me, "Where do you think your brain is?"

I responded quickly, "It's in my head."

"Exactly! You have had a severe car accident, and your body is going through the repair process. It first repaired your foot. Then it repaired your leg. It has started to repair your arm, and it will finally begin repairing your head and your brain. I will tell you right now reconstructing your brain and regaining your memory will be one of the hardest things you have ever done."

I fervently asked her, "Well, can we please focus on repairing that? I am seriously misconstructed, and I want to be able to remember again."

"Yes, we can work on that."

When I finished my therapy sessions with Mrs. Sheri, I had to concentrate on speech therapy and was instructed to meet with Mrs. Tatiana, a speech therapist. During our brief first meeting, I told her about the conversation I previously had with Mrs. Sheri. I told her of all the struggles I was going through because of my car accident. I ask her if she would please work on my memory recuperation so I could just be normal again. She looked me in my eyes and politely yet firmly stated, "I know. That is what we do in speech therapy in a rehabilitation hospital. We work with you so that you will be able to be normal again."

It may have been an ignorant   question, but I really just wanted to work on my memory and my head so I could walk away from this accident and pretend like it never happened. I wanted to be able to act like everyone else acted, like I acted before the accident. I asked her if there was anything I could do to speed up the process.

6

LIFE-CHANGING MOMENT

I continued to see Mrs. Sheri and Mrs. Tatiana, among other therapists, as an outpatient at the rehabilitation hospital. I also had to see several physical therapists who were giving me specific instructions that would eventually help me achieve certain exercises to aid in repairing the injuries affecting my movements.

The speech therapist, Mrs. Tatiana, was one of the few therapists who gave me homework assignments to work on between sessions. I was so thankful to have the opportunity to do so. During one session she told me that I was finishing all the homework assignments rather quickly, that I had the tendency to rush through my homework assignments once I returned to my parents' house in El Paso.

I then began to realize something that I tended to do each time I had homework. I purposefully tried to finish all the homework that was given to me in under an hour. I was getting exceedingly good at it. And it really did not matter how many homework sheets Mrs. Tatiana gave me.

On one occasion Mrs. Tatiana was kind enough to ask me how I was doing with all the homework she had been giving me. In then I told her I effortlessly finished all the homework assignments sheets in under an hour. She then began to laugh and told me, "No, that is not how you're supposed to be doing it. This time I will give you at least six assignments. I want you to pick two assignments and finish them on Friday. Then pick two other assignments, and try to finish them on Saturday. Finally, I know that you are currently going to church, but if you can, try finishing them on Sunday before or after church. If you are not able to finish them on Sunday, then finish the final two assignments on Monday to be able to stimulate your brain. And do not forget to read a book. When you read a book, it will stimulate your brain. With proper time and consistent effort, you will be able to regain your full memory as it once was."

I was marveled by all the information that she gave me. Though I wanted to regain my memory and for my brain to be fully reconstructed, I was not doing the assignments properly and possibly hindering my recovery. I went home and divided up my assignments based on which day I would finish them. I was amazed by the idea she shared about reading a book. After dividing the assignments, I wondered if I could discover any books at my parents' house that I would like to read as Mrs. Tatiana had recommended.

After spending many hours trying to locate such books, I was able to find three. Two of them were written by Paulo Coelho. The third book was called *Crazy Love* by the author Francis Chan. At that time I could not remember anything about Francis Chan. My brain was so severely damaged that I did not recall traveling to Kansas City to hear him preach. I did remember that before the accident, I had read several different books by Paulo Coelho. Of the two that I could remember previously reading, only one was a great read; the other was average at best.

Though I had no memory of Francis Chan, I decided to begin with *Crazy Love*. I did not contemplate whether it was as an excellent book or an average book.. Once I finished reading that book, I would proceed with reading a book by Coelho. I came to the conclusion that if I wanted to reconstruct my brain and remember once again, I needed to begin reading many types of books.

When I began reading *Crazy Love*, I have not a doubt that the Holy Spirit was with me. I came to a specific part of the book where it began to state something similar to don't ask yourself where should you go or what should you do or what you need to accomplish? Those questions made me consider how I used to live my life. My grandfather had died of old age just a couple of months before my accident, and then I had a near-fatal accident. In the moment of that realization, I thought of a lesson that I learned while working on my bachelor's degree in business administration.

One marketing concept I learned, was that nothing in life is free. You must earn anything that you have in life. I began to contemplate that heaven must fall under the same concept and concluded that heaven definitely had to fall under the same category. I then began to rationalize within myself that I had to earn my way into heaven as well.

I then considered my life. I believed I had to have earned at or somewhere near 75 percent of my way to heaven. I reasoned that I had accomplished this because I was previously a missionary in Veracruz, Mexico. I was even one of the few people who were given the opportunity and responsibility to be in charge of leading the worship team. On some occasions, the pastor asked me to give the sermon in the church while he traveled back to the United States for a number of weeks. And I had accomplished that task on several occasions.

I still, however, needed another 25 percent. I questioned how I would be able to earn the last 25 percent. I had previously heard a sermon by Ravi Zacharias, a man who had become one of the most famous and well-known modern apologists. I reasoned that all I needed to do was to gain a doctorate in theology and apologetics, so I could be remarkably similar to him. I believed that having died after accomplishing all these difficult tasks, God would tell me, "OK, you have earned your way into heaven."

All these thoughts continuously raced through my head while I read *Crazy Love*. But then Francis Chan changed his direction and said, "The real question you should ask yourself is the question 'Why does Jesus love you?'" When I read that phrase, tears began to fall. I quickly finished that particular chapter.

After finishing that chapter, I rushed to another room and began to cry. I cried and cried without any remorse or pause. I simply could not stop crying because Jesus just simply loved me. I came to the realization that He did not ask about my accomplishments or the distinct trajectory I had previously taken. The only thing that was important was that Jesus loved me. I just cried and cried.

I began to remember how Jesus had come to this world born through a virgin. Jesus was raised as any ordinary child. Yet he taught Pharisees and Sadducees time and time again in the temple while still a child. He was ultimately betrayed by Judas Iscariot and tortured, nailed to a cross between two others being crucified at the same time. Jesus was buried, and on the third day, He rose from the dead. Jesus did all this not because He wanted to demonstrate something, prove something, or ridicule anyone. Jesus went through this punishment for one simple reason: Because He simply loves me. Not only does He love me, He loves everyone else as well.

I will never forget that this occurred to me in June 2019. The next day I began to confess all my sins. I did not feel worthy enough to simply say, "Jesus, forgive me of all my sins." No, I began to confess all my sins one at a time. I mentioned the names of those I committed the sins with. I named the locations where I committed the sins. I even mentioned the money I used to commit the distinct, innumerous sins.

After I had finished confessing, I asked Jesus, "Would You please forgive me?" I seriously thought that He was going to react in anger, as my earthly father would do. I thought that He might belittle me. I thought He would respond, "Really? You are asking Me and telling Me to grant you some forgiveness even after I saved you from a horrific car accident. And you still have the audacity to ask for forgiveness?" I seriously thought that He was going to raise His hand and attempt to slap me across the face.

I was thinking about how I would react if He responded in how I feared. I began to come up with counterreactions I could use in response. I thought I could defend myself with, "OK, God, I'll go through the accident again if I have to! You can even chop off my leg or cut my arm off if You have to! Do whatever You have to do to me, but please, please Lord, please just forgive me."

Yet He responded to me in the gentlest manner. "It is OK, son. I forgive you. Just go, and sin no more."

After His response, I emphatically raised my hands toward the sky and began telling myself, "Yes! He did not get angry like my father used to get angry or even punish me any further—which I deserved—after I confessed to Him all my sins. I felt happy and excited in that moment.

But within a matter of seconds, I began to get quiet. I was utterly surprised to contemplate what I had just experienced, and I was genuinely amazed the remarkable love, kindness, and forgiveness that He had just shown me. I could not comprehend how, with all His knowledge and understanding of the things that I had previously done, He still decided to show His forgiveness by demonstrating His love and mercy toward me.

7

FINAL THOUGHTS

After considering everything I recently experienced on all these remarkable occasions, I was still able to have a remarkable life-changing moment. During that month I was beginning to enter my final weeks of rehabilitation, which provided me with many excellent services. I became completely aware that eventually these events would lead me to my final days of having to be at the rehabilitation hospital in Las Cruces.

In that moment I had a friend who stopped being my friend and became just an acquaintance ask me, "How do you feel about all this and the whole situation? You nearly died being involved in a very severe, life-threatening car accident. How do feel about all of it? Not only were you involved in a very severe car accident, you had to go to a rehabilitation hospital. At the rehabilitation hospital, you had to work hard so that you could even be able to walk and think like a normal person. The person who nearly killed you totaled your car. How do you feel about all this?"

While looking at the ground, I responded, "I am really glad that it all happened to me. It was the best thing that could ever have happened to me. It was better than I could have ever wished for. More than I could have ever imagined."

He quickly asked, "Why would you say that?"

I lifted my head, looked him straight in his eyes, and responded, "I am happy that it all happened to me because I actually met Jesus."

He quickly entered debate fashion already, wanting to argue with me about what I said. You see, I knew that he was going to begin his argument by stating that I had been going to a specific church for countless years. On one occasion I even had the opportunity to be a missionary in a foreign country. I had extensive knowledge about knowing precisely who God is. If he wanted to, he could have alleged how I even heard of and memorized many scriptures throughout the Bible, and question how I just met Jesus.

So that I would not have to enter a perilous debate with him, I quickly told him I had to leave. He responded arrogantly, "Where are you going? We were just about to enter into an intriguing conversation."

I responded, "I have to go at this precise moment. It is actually better if I leave now, before I begin to forget anything, like I previously had to suffer through." To be honest, I simply did not want to have to explain to him the difference between knowing *about* God and completely knowing Him as a person and committing your life to Him.

With that being said, I want to finish off this book with a specific homework assignment for each of you. I am not trying to leave you with this assignment because I want to enter into a theological discussion or even a spiritual matter. I am simply leaving you with this assignment for one simple purpose: I do not want any human being to have to go through the same severe tragedy that I experienced in order to ask yourself this question.

So more than just trying to be a man of encouragement, I want to challenge each of you to ask yourself, "Do I know about God just like Sonny did prior to his accident? Sonny was a particular person who could boastfully say that he knew about God, whether it be intellectually, psychologically, or even spiritually because he knew exactly who God was and about Him.

"Or do I know Him in person, and have I committed my life to Him just like Sonny did after his severe car accident?"

I leave you with this assignment because the answers that will be given to both those questions will ultimately affect you and determine if you will end up going to heaven or hell. I was involved in a near-fatal, life-changing car accident. If I had died, I would not have gone to heaven. Where would I have ended up going? I will leave that question for you as part of the homework assignment.

Thank you for reading my book about the life-changing moment that I had to experience. May God bless you.

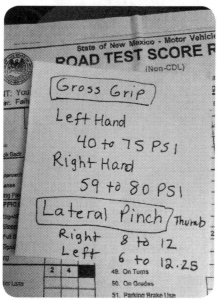

Printed in the United States
by Baker & Taylor Publisher Services